Kingdom Living
Small Group Series

Six Habits
of Highly Effective Christians

Kingdom Living
Small Group Series

Six Habits of Highly Effective Christians

ampelōn
PUBLISHING

ISBN: 978-0-9786394-2-6

Printed in the United States of America
First printing

Requests for information should be addressed to:
Ampelon Publishing
6920 Jimmy Carter Blvd., Suite 200
Norcross, GA 30071
To order other Ampelon Publishing products, visit us on the web at:
www.ampelonpublishing.com

Contents

THE KINGDOM LIVING BIBLE STUDY SERIES

The kingdom of God is not defined by mighty fortress walls, colorful pennants fluttering in the breeze, or mounted saints on powerful steeds. It's not a place where sentries patrol castle walls and moats deter intruders. The kingdom of God isn't a place we can visit, but it's as real as any empire known to man.

The kingdom of God is really a kingdom within a kingdom. It's a spiritual kingdom, ushered in by Jesus, where God reigns over everything. It is both a present reality and a future hope. And yet it exists in the midst of the kingdoms of this earth, where Satan rules.

The Israelites had been promised this kingdom of God, also referred to as the kingdom of heaven in the book of Matthew. They had been waiting thousands of years for the promised King who would restore them to power and save them from their suffering. So when John the Baptist proclaimed, "Repent, for the kingdom of heaven is near" (Matthew 3:2), they listened.

Jesus said those same words Himself in Matthew 4:17. In fact, the message of the kingdom of God was the reason Jesus said He came. When the people of Capernaum wanted Jesus to stay longer, He said, "I must preach the good news of the kingdom of God to the other towns also, because that is why I was sent" (Luke 4:43). Christianity did not start with the story of the resurrection of Jesus—that hadn't happened. People repented and turned to God through the teachings and the reality of the kingdom of heaven.

Jesus modeled the life of a subject of the kingdom of heaven. As He walked from city to city, He invested His life in others, taught, preached the good news of the kingdom, cared for the poor, healed the sick, and cast out demons. Jesus showed us that the kingdom of God is where God's Word is being taught and His work is being done.

As believers today, we are called to continue the works of Jesus and advance the kingdom of God. Jesus said, "Truly, truly, I say to you, he who believes in Me, the works that I do, he will do also; and greater works than these he will do; because I go to the Father" (John 14:12, NASB). However, as people of the Kingdom, we are also thrust into a war with God's enemies. How do we obey the commands of Jesus, yet battle an unseen enemy?

The key to walking in the power of the kingdom of God is learning to do what the Father is doing in each situation. Jesus Himself acknowledged His dependence on God: "Therefore Jesus answered and was saying to them, 'Truly, truly, I say to you, the Son can do nothing of Himself, unless it is something He sees the Father doing; for whatever the Father does, these things the Son also does in like manner'" (John 5:19, NASB).

In this Kingdom Living Bible Study Series, we will delve deeply into what living life as a follower of Jesus is all about. We'll study Scripture and apply the Word of God to our hearts and lives. We'll learn how to live like Christ, how to watch for what the Father is doing, experience transformation, and impact our community with the Good News of the Gospel.

Life in the kingdom of God is exciting! We invite you to pursue following Jesus with all your heart and get ready for an adventure. Kingdom living will transform your life.

Small Group Tips

These studies are designed for personal or group studies. If you are participating in a group, we would like to share some tips for making it a great experience.

First, congratulations on taking this step to develop community with other believers! We weren't meant to be isolated Christians. After Pentecost, there were 3,000 believers in Jerusalem. Acts 2:42 says, "They devoted themselves to the apostles' teaching and to the fellowship, to the breaking of bread and to prayer." Imagine 3,000 believers, passionate about their love for God, meeting in homes for fellowship, teaching and prayer. Oh, yes, ... and food!

Small groups were one of the first ways the kingdom of God was advanced. Acts 2:46-47 tells us more about these first believers: "Every day they continued to meet together in the temple courts. They broke bread in their homes and ate together with glad and sincere hearts, praising God and enjoying the favor of all the people. And the Lord added to their number daily those who were being saved." Meeting in large groups, meeting in homes in small groups, praising God and sharing the Good News—what an amazing picture of community.

As you embark on this study, we encourage you to open your heart to what God might want to do during your small group time. Here are some ideas on how to prepare:

1. Before each group meeting, do your best to be prepared—pray about and get familiar with the content of that week's Bible study.

2. Pray for your group beforehand. Pray for your leaders, the hosts, and the other people in the group.

3. Watch for God to speak to you during the small group. This could be during worship, prayer, through another member of the group, or quietly in your heart.

4. Be open to meeting with people different from you. God may specifically put you in a group so you can learn from others with different experiences and insights.

5. Be transparent. You don't have to spill your guts, but be willing to share your personal struggles when appropriate. This is how trust develops in a group.

6. Be yourself. God has called you into His service just how you are. You don't have to try and be like anybody else. Guard your heart against comparisons.

7. Protect confidentiality. What is shared in the group, stays in the group.

8. Look for one idea to apply to your life today. Allow God's Word to change your life one small step at a time.

Bible Study Basics

Studying the Bible can seem overwhelming. It doesn't have to be. Our goal with this series is to learn more about life in the kingdom of God bit by bit. God wants us to understand His Word and will open our ears and hearts when we approach Bible study with a willing heart. Here are some tips to get you started:

1. Pray before doing your lesson. Ask God to teach you from the Scriptures and to speak to you through the Holy Spirit.

2. Read the Scripture reference several times. If it's a familiar verse, read it out loud to gain a new perspective. Read it in different versions if you have them. (www.biblegateway.com and www.crosswalk.com offer many versions on line)

3. If you have a Bible with study notes, read them. Read any cross-references (often indicated by a small letter after a word).

4. Read with expectancy that God will teach you from His Word. Don't try to make the Scripture say what you want it to say.

5. Look for the main theme of each passage, look for the context (read before and after the verse), and identify how the central truth applies to you.

6. Answer the questions to the best of your ability. If you are unsure of an answer, that's OK. Share that with the group and ask for their help in understanding the passage or question.

7. Thank God for the gift of the Bible and for teaching you through it.

We pray that God will touch you in a deep and intimate way as you study His word and apply yourself to becoming a passionate follower of Jesus. May God bless you richly.

Six Habits of Highly Effective Christians

Imagine a good friend calls Friday afternoon and says, "Dave, I've got tickets to a concert tomorrow night. It starts at 7 p.m. Are you free?" You answer, "I sure am! I'd love to go. I'll see you then!" You hang up the phone and go about the rest of your day.

On Saturday, you are getting ready to leave and, all of a sudden, you realize you never asked for any details—like which concert he meant, or where it was being performed. You are dressed, car keys in hand, and no idea which direction to go. When you don't show up, your friend is going to be worried, disappointed, or mad—possibly all three. He doesn't have a cell phone, so there's no way to contact him for more details. You turn away from the door, toss your coat on a chair. and slump down on the couch in disappointment.

Sounds like a bad dream, right? How could anyone accept an invitation to a wonderful event without learning more? The possibility of a great evening with a friend is just beyond your reach, but you can't make it happen. You've got the means to drive there, but you don't know the way.

We've all been invited to something wonderful—life with Jesus. And yet how many of us accept the invitation and then don't show up for the event? When that happens, we only taste a small part of the joy God longs for us to experience. Jesus said He came so that we would have life. Not a partial life, not a beaten and battered life, but a full and abundant life. In John 10:10 Jesus said, "The thief comes only to steal and kill and destroy; I came that they may have life, and have it abundantly" (NASB).

Unfortunately, we have an enemy who wants us to have a partial life. Satan would like our life to be like a tree eaten by bark beetles or a leaf nibbled by a worm. He picks away at us until we meander around, filled with disappointment and regret. Satan would like us to stay lost and never find our way to abundant life.

To experience a full and rich Christian life, we need to pay attention to the details of our invitation. Saying "yes" to Jesus is just the beginning of our lives as Christians. In order to grow in our faith and become mature Christians, there are certain things we need to do.

This study addresses six of the most important disciplines for every Christian: reading the Bible, praying, obeying God's commands, giving, living in community with others, and serving. As you invest time in becoming a more effective Christian, you'll experience a renewed excitement for your faith. God will speak directly to you and use you to advance the Kingdom of God in ways you've never experienced. Your Christian walk will explode with a renewed passion for Jesus, and you'll have overflowing joy.

That's the abundant life Jesus wants to bring each of us, and we have all the details and directions we need right in front of us. Let's get started!

One

KNOW THE BIBLE

Getting acquainted with our owner's manual for life

All Scripture is inspired by God and profitable for teaching, for reproof, for correction, for training in righteousness; so that the man of God may be equipped for every good work.

2 Timothy 3:16-17 (NASB)

Very few people buy a new car and rush home to read the owner's manual. If you're like most of us, the most popular time to read the owner's manual of a car is when you've got a flat tire or a weird light pops up on the dashboard. Then you are glued to each page of that little book. The reality is, other than times of trouble, the owner's manual of most cars sits safely tucked in a glove compartment.

We've got another owner's manual that needs to be read more than in times of trouble—and that's the Bible. The Bible is our manual for life; it's God's guide for each of us. There's not a page of the Bible that can't help us figure out some aspect of this life. The Bible shows us what pleases and displeases God. It gives us guidelines for getting along with others, managing money, succeeding at work and school, and teaches us how to develop the most important relationship in our lives: our relationship with God.

The Word of God is the works of God recorded by men and women inspired by the Holy Spirit. It's a collection of stories about people who had life experiences with God—ordinary people who saw His miracles, who learned to trust Him, who were redeemed from darkness, who were forgiven great sin, who were raised from the dead, and who were used to bring glory to God.

One of the most important things about the Bible is it's the truth! The whole truth! Not relative truth, not what was true for some people or true for another generation—but God's timeless truth. Jesus said this about the truth, "... if you hold to my teaching, you are really my disciples. Then you will know the truth, and the truth will set you free" (John 8:31b-32). What a promise! When we know the truth, we will be free from the bondage of lies. But we have to read the truth to know the truth.

Get into the habit of reading your Bible daily. Start by choosing one book of the Bible. Maybe you'd like to read Genesis and learn about the creation of the world. Or pick Matthew and learn about Jesus' life on earth. Once you've decided on a book of the Bible to read, then read at least one chapter a day. Read it again if you didn't understand parts. God wants you to understand the Bible. If you've had trouble understanding the Bible in the past, then pray and ask God to help you understand what you read. Pray Psalm 119:18: "Open my eyes Lord that I may behold wonderful things from Thy Law" (NASB).

In this session we'll be looking at four reasons why it's important to read the Bible: to know God, to know truth, to develop our convictions, and to sharpen our skills. Our hope is that through this study, you will be inspired to start, or continue, a lifetime of reading the Bible.

Let's Talk

1) When you were a child, did you have a favorite story? What was it?

2) What's one of the best books you've read as an adult? Why did you like it?

Entering In

BytheWay ...

The Bible is divided into two parts. The Old Testament starts with the creation of the world. The New Testament starts with the birth of Jesus. God's character never changes. That means the whole Bible is important, as it helps us learn more about who God really is – not a fictional character.

WE CAN KNOW GOD BY READING THE BIBLE.
Read 1 John 2:3-6.

3) According to this passage, what is proof that we know God?

· When we obey his commands
· when we obey his word, God's love is truly made complete in him

4) How does obeying God's commands help us know God?

it helps us know what is His heart.
Jesus obeyed God's commands... we must walk as though Jesus did...
for this will lead us into God's heart

5) What are some things we learn about God's nature by reading the Bible?

God loves so much... even enemies
God is generous
God is forgiving
God is kind, gentle, self-controlled, holy, pure, wise, joy, peace
faithful, do not worry, give to poor.

We can know the truth.

Read Psalm 119:160.

All your words are TRUE, all your righteous laws are eternal.

6) In today's world, name some examples of contradictory truths people believe?

7) What are some differences between eternal Truth and "truth" that doesn't last?

8) List some dangers of taking scripture out of context, or only knowing parts of the Bible?

contradiction, false when out of context.

We develop our convictions.

Read Hebrews 5:14.

9) How do you define a conviction?

Strong belief.

10) On what do most people base their convictions?

feelings

11) Based on this scripture, what are some steps to developing biblical convictions?

milk (elementary truths) → solid food

constant use/practice → training →

discernment b/w evil + good.

12) Name one conviction you hold that has come from reading God's word?

All of God's word is TRUE.

THE BIBLE COMMANDS US TO ACT.
Read James 1:22-25.

13) How might those who only hear God's word delude or deceive themselves?

Action / DO what the word says.
Just hearing it does not change / bless us.

14) When you are a "doer" of the word, what happens inside your heart?

frees us → blesses us.

Putting Feet to It

15) What has been the biggest benefit to you personally from reading the Bible?

connects me to the heart of God & draws me closer. strengthens + encourages me.

16) What is your biggest challenge in reading the Bible?

Discipline - I tend to allow other distractions get in the way.

Taking It with You

Matthew 6:33: "But seek first his kingdom and his righteousness, and all these things will be given to you as well." (NASB)

Journal

Two

MAKE PRAYER A PRIORITY

Connecting with the heart of God

Be joyful always; pray continually; give thanks in all circumstances, for this is God's will for you in Christ Jesus.

1 Thessalonians 5:16-18

Prayer can change our lives and the lives of others. Even though prayer is a powerful tool for an effective Christian, it is often misunderstood and underused. Many Christians simply don't understand why they should pray, or even how to pray.

The disciples knew they needed to learn more about prayer. In Luke 11:1, the disciples asked Jesus to teach them to pray. They wanted to learn how to pray like Jesus prayed. What did the disciples see in Jesus' prayer life that prompted them to want to learn more? Was it the language Jesus used? Maybe He was using deep theological terms. Was it His physical posture when He prayed? Maybe He moved His arms and legs in a certain way. It's more likely the disciples saw the depth of spiritual relationship Jesus had with His Heavenly Father, and they saw what happened when Jesus prayed—and they wanted the same.

Jesus responds to the disciples' question with what we call the Lord's Prayer. Its simplicity shows that anyone can pray like Jesus:

> "He said to them, 'When you pray, say: Father, hallowed be your name, your kingdom come. Give us each day our daily bread. Forgive us our sins, for we also forgive everyone who sins against us. And lead us not into temptation.'" (Luke 11:2-4)

The truth is there's nothing more vital to our Christian life than prayer. The problem is many Christians know more about the latest primetime reality show than they know about prayer. There's much more to prayer than can be covered in one Bible study session. However, it's our hope that this will inspire you to learn more about this lifeline to God.

Let's Talk

1) When you have a problem, whom do you call first for help? (Name a person.) Why?

2) Have you ever thought you were in control of a situation, only to discover at some point you weren't in control at all? Describe the situation.

Entering In

PRAYER SHOWS OUR DEPENDENCE ON GOD.

Read John 15:5.

3) Jesus conveys the importance of abiding in Him through the analogy of a vine and branches. What are some characteristics of vines and branches? If you aren't familiar with a vineyard, use any plant that has a trunk and branches as your example.

ByTheWay ...

The word "abide" or "remain" is the Greek word meno. It conveys the idea of tarrying, or staying in a place. To stay somewhere, we first have to get there. Then, we have the choice of leaving quickly or resting awhile. Jesus is calling us to remain with Him, not quickly pray or read His Word then forget about Him. We are called to stay connected at all times.

4) What are some ways we can abide in Christ?

5) Knowing we can do nothing without Christ, how should that change your prayer life?

6) How does thinking we don't need God's help impact our prayer life?

PRAYER IS GOD'S CHOSEN METHOD FOR MEETING OUR NEEDS. Read Philippians 4:6-7.

By the Way ...

This passage in Philippians mentions two ways to present concerns to God: prayer and petition. Are they the same thing? Are they different? The original Greek words are different, with slightly different meanings. The NIV Bible Commentary says this, "'Prayer' denotes the petitioner's attitude of mind as worshipful. 'Petition' denotes prayers as expressions of need." This means we should praise God for who He is, and then ask for what we need.

7) According to this passage, how should we handle our concerns?

8) What types of problems in our lives should we present to God?

9) How do worry and anxiety affect our faith?

10) What are some needs you currently have that you have neglected to ask God's help with?

Prayer is how we can cooperate with God to accomplish His plan for the world.

Read John 14:12-13.

11) Jesus speaks with confidence about the works His disciples will do when He's gone. Considering that we are disciples of Jesus, what should we be doing? Give some examples.

12) According to this passage, what is the key to this happening in our lives?

Putting Feet to It

13) What are some hindrances that prevent you from developing a more effective prayer life? Share these hurdles with someone. Brainstorm some possible solutions.

14) Consider the needs in your sphere of influence. What are some things God might want to do through your prayers?

Taking It with You

Matthew 21:22: "And all things you ask in prayer, believing, you will receive." (NASB)

Journal

Three

LIVE A LIFE OF OBEDIENCE

Learning to obey God ... even when it's tough

But Samuel replied: "Does the Lord delight in burnt offerings and sacrifices as much as in obeying the voice of the Lord? To obey is better than sacrifice, and to heed is better than the fat of rams."

1 Samuel 15:22

Most parents love their children with equal measure. But when they want to get something important delivered to the school office, they know which one will get it there in one piece. They know which one will look for a sibling on a playground full of children until he's found, and which one will get distracted by the swings and abandon the search. Basically, parents know which child will obey their request, even when it's difficult.

Of course, children will be children, and most grow out of silly distractions and a preference for play. Few kids are born with a bent toward obedience. But when a child chooses to be obedient, parents will often give that child more responsibility and entrust him or her with things of greater value.

Does God look at us the same way? Does He decide whom He can trust with something important based on our obedience? In Matthew 25, we read a story Jesus told showing God does care about our obedience, and as we obey Him, He trusts us with more.

Many Christians want more of the right things. They want to know more of God. They want more joy in their lives. They want to do more things for the sake of Jesus. They want to be entrusted with more responsibility. They would like to have more money to give away. And sometimes they question why they don't have more.

When that happens, the question every Christian needs to ask is "Have I been obedient with what God has already asked me to do?" Have you served God even when it was hard? Have you been faithful with money when you had little? Have you opened your home to others even though it seemed too small? How obedient have you already been?

Jesus showed us God's heart about obedience in the parable of the talents found in Matthew 25. The servants in the story were entrusted with "talents" or a unit of money. Two invested what they had and were able to offer a profit back to their master when he returned from his trip. The story describes the happiness of the master when his servants proved themselves faithful. In response to their obedience, the master was willing to give them more. Verse 21 reads:

> "His master replied, 'Well done, good and faithful servant! You have been faithful with a few things; I will put you in charge of many things. Come and share your master's happiness!'"

God is looking at us to see how faithful we are with what He has given us. We each have an amount of intelligence, personal skills, physical strength, and emotional reserve. For most of us, we've been given shelter, food, and a portion of money. We are each asked to serve God with what we've been given. Then God waits to see how obedient we will be.

There are many other rewards for being obedient than just getting more responsibility. Knowing we've pleased God brings its own joy. Another great reward is playing a part in advancing the Kingdom of God here on earth. Our obedience shows Jesus how much we love Him, and frees us from slavery to sin.

Obedience doesn't come naturally. It takes saying "yes" to God hundreds of times in the little things. When we are obedient, we experience God's pleasure. In this session, we'll look at some scriptures about obedience and consider how it can help us become more effective Christians.

Let's Talk

1) Can you remember getting into trouble as a child? What was one way you disobeyed your parents?

2) Think of someone you know who doesn't come close to fulfilling his or her potential in life. What are some of the reasons this happens?

Entering In

1 Corinthians 4:2: "Now it is required that those who have been given a trust must prove faithful."

Read Matthew 25:14-30.

3) What task did the master in this story assign his three slaves/servants?

4) Based on the master's response to each of the servants, what did the master expect them to do with the talents?

5) How does the master react to each of the servants?

ByTheWay ...

There are three ways people can respond when asked to fulfill an assignment: 1) accusers will blame others, 2) excusers will find a reason why they couldn't get something done, and 3) choosers will assume responsibility and finish the assignment.

6) What excuses does the third servant give for not being faithful with his talent?

7) Another reason the third servant might have disobeyed his master is that he minimized the importance of one talent. What are some of the responsibilities we've been given and minimized their importance?

Read Matthew 21:28-32.

8) What does this parable tell us about the importance of believing Jesus and being obedient?

9) What might have been in the heart of the second son, who said "yes" but then didn't obey?

10) Identify something you know God wants you to do, but you haven't done.

11) Examine your heart. Why have you delayed obeying?

12) What is Jesus' point in telling this parable?

BytheWay ...

Miracles almost always start when someone does something very ordinary in obedience to God.

Read John 14:21.

13) What does Jesus say about those who obey His commands?

14) Why does obedience show our love for Jesus?

15) What commands of Jesus are hardest for you to obey?

16) What help do you need to be more obedient to God?

Read Romans 6:16-18.

17) This passage contrasts two options for our obedience. Describe our two choices.

18) When we choose obedience, what is our reward? What does that look like in a Christian's life?

Putting Feet to It

19) Obedience to God is a choice on our part. God does not force us. Why is obedience so important to God?

20) Do you struggle with obeying God's commands in scripture? Pray about what might be the root of your lack of desire to obey. Identify some reasons obedience is difficult for you.

Taking It with You

Matthew 25:21: "His master replied, 'Well done, good and faithful servant! You have been faithful with a few things; I will put you in charge of many things. Come and share your master's happiness!'"

Journal

Four

GIVE TO GOD

Learning to be a good steward of your finances

One man gives freely, yet gains even more; another withholds unduly, but comes to poverty.

Proverbs 11:24

Imagine walking into church one day to discover all your financial information on display. Your check register is copied as a bulletin insert. Your bank statement is in a Power Point presentation, and the pastor somehow got records of how you spent your cash. Some people would immediately sprint out the back door, horrified at the thought of their spending habits being exposed!

Why is money, and how we spend it, such a big deal? It's a big deal because we intuitively know you can tell a lot about a person by how he or she spends money. The entries in our check register reveal clues about who we really are.

The way we handle money—how we earn it, how we spend it, and how we give it away—shows what's important to us. Do we spend money on items that satisfy for a short while, or do we invest in things of eternal value? Our checkbooks tell the truth about what we value.

For a Christian, the way we handle money also shows how we feel about God. It shows whether God is really important to us or not. Our spending and giving habits reveal whether we worship God with just our words or also with our resources.

Though many of us are uncomfortable talking about money, the Bible has over 2,000 verses referring to it. God knows that how we manage this necessary part of life is important to being an effective Christian. Managing our money the way God wants us to shows our commitment to obeying Him in all areas of our lives –

especially those areas few see. When we give back to God a portion of what He has given us, we learn to put God first in our lives. We also become more like God when we give, because God gives freely.

Holding on to our money with an open hand shows we trust God. God has given us everything we have: our health, our jobs, our homes, and our financial resources. Giving back to God shows we trust that His Word is true, and we trust Him to provide for our needs.

At the very heart of the whole issue of giving money to God is whether or not God can be trusted. The answer is "yes!" God can be trusted. Especially in the area of money and giving.

Let's Talk

1) Have you ever bought something you later regretted? What was it?

2) If someone were to look at your check register or credit card statement, what would they say is important to you?

Entering In

We give to be obedient.

ByTheWay ...

The word "tithe" comes from the Hebrew word meaning "tenth part." God's people were asked to return to God at least ten percent of what they earned. The first biblical reference to giving ten percent in honor of God is found in Genesis 14. Abram gave one-tenth of the spoils of war to Melchizedek, the priest-king of Salem, after God delivered Abram's enemies into his hands.

Read Malachi 3:1-12.

3) How had the Israelites disobeyed God?

4) What are some reasons God would want His people to give ten percent of their income to His purposes?

5) The storehouse referred to in Malachi 3:10 was the temple, their place of worship. Why might God ask that our tithes be given to our place of worship – the local church?

ByTheWay ...

The storehouse for the Israelites at that time was the temple. It served as a warehouse for all the tithes of the people, such as produce or livestock. The Levites were responsible for managing and distributing the collected tithes. They used the tithe to support the priest and workers of the temple. It also was used as there was need in the community.

6) When we are obedient to God in our tithes, what is His promise to us?

We give to proclaim God is first in our lives.

The purpose of tithing is to teach you always to put God first in your lives.

— Deuteronomy 14:23b, LB

ByTheWay ...

In the first of the Ten Commandments, God says, "You shall have no other gods before me." God is saying, "Put me first – make me number one in your life." In today's world, a "god" can be anything in your life that controls you, or anything you turn to on a regular basis for comfort besides God. This can be a person, relationship, substance, or even entertainment. For many of us, money controls us, brings comfort, and comes before God.

7) As Christians, what are different practical ways we show that God is first in our lives?

8) How does money sometimes take first place in our lives?

9) Why would obeying God with our money teach us to "put God first"?

We give to declare the location of our hearts.

Read Matthew 6:19-21.

10) What types of things do we spend money on that God would consider earthly treasures?

11) What are some examples of heavenly treasures we can accumulate here on earth?

12) How does our choice of treasure (earthly or heavenly) affect our attitude toward life? Toward God?

By the Way ...

Our "heart" is the center of our spiritual and physical life, making it sort of the "engine" of our spiritual life. Consequently, our heart will lead us. This passage in Matthew 6, however, shows us that where we invest our finances determines which direction our heart will go.

Putting Feet to It

13) If you had to declare your master based on your checkbook, would it be God or money?

14) What are some practical ways you can change your earning, spending, and giving habits to make God first in your life?

Taking It with You

Matthew 6:19-21: "Do not store up for yourselves treasures on earth, where moth and rust destroy, and where thieves break in and steal. But store up for yourselves treasures in heaven, where neither moth nor rust destroys, and where thieves do not break in or steal; for where your treasure is, there your heart will be also." (NASB)

Journal

Five

LIVE IN COMMUNITY

Experiencing the power of life together

"This is My commandment, that you love one another, just as I have loved you."

John 15:12

A tragedy happened in our church a few years ago—a young woman was killed in a car accident. The shock rippled through the church and hearts of all who knew and loved this woman. The woman, her parents, two of her aunts, and their families were active members at our church.

What happened within hours of her death is why living in community is so important. It didn't take long for the news to circulate, and when it did, people leapt into action. The parents of this young lady led a small group, and those members immediately surrounded them with love, brought food, cleaned their house, sent cards and letters, took over their responsibilities at church, helped with their home-based business and more. The care extended beyond the group they led to people at church who hardly knew them, but who were moved with compassion.

The grief felt by the family was overwhelming for a long time. One of the beautiful things to happen was their Christian brothers and sisters stayed faithful throughout the next year to support them in very practical ways, and it still continues today.

In a world where people feel isolated and alone, God has created a unique and loving community called the church. In fact, one of the first acts in Jesus' ministry was to establish a community of believers, the disciples. These 13 men, including Jesus, transformed the world with the Good News of the kingdom of God. Throughout His ministry, Jesus modeled and taught about life in this new kind of community.

We were not created to do life or ministry alone. Community was God's plan to change the world. Jesus was completely capable of preaching, teaching, and healing by Himself. It's not that Jesus needed anyone to help Him, but God designed us to need each other. Jesus lived this out by taking along twelve friends.

Being in a loving community helps us in many ways. We have friends to encourage us when we feel down, someone to help us when we struggle with a problem. We learn to love like Jesus loved. Community helps us stay committed to our Christian faith, and creates a safe environment where we can be ourselves. There are many more benefits to being involved in a Christian community, but one of the best is that Jesus is uniquely present when we gather. Wherever Jesus is, is a good place to be!

If you are doing this study as part of a small group, or within a church, you are already in a Christian community. May this study inspire you to become more involved in your small group and church, and experience all God has for you through this wonderful thing called community.

Let's Talk

1) When you and your friends get together, what do you like to do best?

2) Have you ever been part of a small group of people, either working toward a goal, or just being friends? What did you like best about being a member of that group?

Entering In

COMMUNITY HELPS US ENCOURAGE EACH OTHER.

Read Hebrews 10:24-25.

3) How does meeting together, either in a small group or church setting, help us encourage each other?

4) Just meeting together doesn't guarantee there will be a sense of community. What are some attributes of a healthy Christian community?

5) How can Christians spur one another toward love and good deeds? Identify some practical ways this can happen.

ByTheWay ...

The word "spur" is an interesting choice for the writer of Hebrews. It brings to mind a horse rider with spurs strapped to his boots. The spurs are intended to be an irritant to the horse, thereby "encouraging" an increased speed. While we don't intend to irritate each other—though we sometimes do—we are to be assertive in our encouragement.

Jesus is uniquely present in His community.

Read Matthew 18:20.

6) Jesus said He is present when two or more gather. What is the condition for His presence? What might that mean?

7) Jesus is present with every Christian, whether alone or in a community. Why is Jesus uniquely present when two or more are gathered together?

Being in a community prevents spiritual drift.

Read Proverbs 27:17.

8) For what purpose is iron sharpened?

9) How can Christians "sharpen" each other?

We can be ourselves and receive healing.

Read James 5:16.

10) Why is it difficult to be honest with each other about our weaknesses and sin?

11) What are the different types of healing we can experience when we confess our sins to each other and pray for each other?

12) What is one change you can make in your life to be more transparent and honest with those in your Christian community or small group?

Putting Feet to It

13) Identify some spiritual growth that has happened to you as a result of being part of a Christian community.

14) What is one way that your Christian community can help you become a more mature believer?

Taking It with You

James 5:16: "Therefore, confess your sins to one another, and pray for one another so that you may be healed. The effective prayer of a righteous man can accomplish much." (NASB)

Journal

Six

SERVE OTHERS

Developing a life of servanthood

"Now that I, your Lord and Teacher, have washed your feet, you also should wash one another's feet. I have set you an example that you should do as I have done for you. I tell you the truth, no servant is greater than his master, nor is a messenger greater than the one who sent him. Now that you know these things, you will be blessed if you do them."

John 13:14-17

Jesus had spent three years with the twelve men seated around the table. They had come to Jerusalem to observe the Passover Feast together. It was an annual event when the Jews remembered how God miraculously freed them from slavery. That night should have been one of celebration, but only Jesus knew the betrayal that was in the heart of one of the men.

Jesus knew He would be leaving His friends, and this would be their final time together. He must have looked at the sun-bronzed faces He loved so dearly, knowing He needed to make this night memorable.

For a moment, imagine you were Jesus. What would you say? What would you do? Many of us might do a review—a highlight of sorts—of the past three years. Maybe touch on the good times and laugh a bit. Or remind the disciples of the most important facts of our teaching. The most organized of us would want them taking notes so they could remember every detail.

That's not at all what Jesus did. With only hours left on earth, Jesus Christ, the Savior of all mankind, quietly rose from the table, wrapped a towel around His waist and washed His disciples' feet. He knelt on the ground, cradled their cracked, smelly feet in His hands, and lovingly washed away the muck and mud with a rag. He moved from friend to friend until all were clean.

They must have been shocked. This was the Son of God. They should be the ones washing His feet. Peter, the bold one, spoke up first. "No" he said. "You shall never wash my feet." Jesus probably expected this particular friend to argue, and was ready with a gentle response. "Unless I wash you, you have no part of me," He said.

One final official teaching and Jesus started the evening by washing feet. What an amazing message. Jesus' actions spoke louder than words. It was clear: we are to serve each other. Not the type of serving that's comfortable. Not the type of serving that's convenient. But the type of selfless serving that gets us down on our hands and knees in the muck and mud of life.

To be an effective Christian, we need to know the Bible, maintain a strong prayer life, obey the commands of God, give of our financial resources, and be an active member of a Christian community. All of these habits are critical to maturing as a Christian, but if we don't serve others in love, we are missing out on the fullness of life in the Kingdom of God. Jesus demonstrated this message with amazing clarity that speaks to us today.

The Apostle Paul wrote these words to summarize God's desire for us:

> You, my brothers, were called to be free. But do not use your freedom to indulge the sinful nature; rather, serve one another in love. The entire law is summed up in a single command: "Love your neighbor as yourself."
>
> —Galatians 5:13-14

Let's Talk

1) Have you ever worked at a service job, such as in a restaurant or retail store? What did you enjoy about that job? What did you dislike?

2) What are some common hindrances to serving others?

Entering In

BytheWay ...

"You were put on earth to make a contribution. You weren't created just to consume resources ... God designed you to make a difference with your life. While many best-selling books offer advice on how to 'get' the most out of life, that's not the reason God made you. You were created to add to life on earth, not just take from it. God wants you to give something back." — Rick Warren, *The Purpose Driven Life*

WE WERE CREATED TO SERVE.

Read Ephesians 2:10.

3) Using Jesus as our example, what types of "good works" should we be doing?

4) God uniquely created you in order to serve. What are some of your natural talents and abilities you can use in serving God?

ByTheWay ...

Our English word "poem" comes from the Greek work translated "workmanship" found in Ephesians 2:10. This conveys the artistic design with which God created each of us. We aren't cookie-cutter imitations; we are original works of art.

SERVING PROVES WE BELONG TO CHRIST.

Read Titus 2:11-14.

5) This passage tells us that Jesus Christ came to do two things. What are they?

6) What is the significance of the order of these two reasons Jesus came?

7) According to this passage, what proves we belong to Jesus? Why would this be proof of our being part of the body of Christ?

In serving others, we serve God.

Read Colossians 3:23-24.

8) How does the knowledge we are actually serving Jesus help when serving is difficult?

9) What types of service are difficult for you? Why?

10) What rewards do we earn when we work at a job for our benefit, or for the benefit of another person?

By the Way …

The washing of feet before a meal was a common practice in ancient Israel, as well as ancient Greece and Rome. A servant was normally assigned the menial task of washing the feet of guests. If a servant wasn't available, the individual would wash his own feet. In some cases, a peer would perform this task for one of equal standing. But never would a teacher perform this task for his disciples. Jesus' humble act defined the heart of a servant leader.

JESUS WAS A SERVANT.

Read John 13:12-17.

11) Summarize Jesus' reason for washing the disciple's feet.

12) What servant attitudes did Jesus demonstrate?

13) Is it more difficult for you to serve or be served? Why?

Putting Feet to It

14) What is keeping you from serving God more fully? What change(s) do you need to make to eliminate that reason?

15) Identify one person you can serve in the coming week. Or, identify one area of service within your local church to which you can commit.

Taking It with You

Colossians 3:23: "Whatever you do, do your work heartily, as for the Lord rather than for men." (NASB)

Journal

leader's guide

one

Know the Bible

Questions One and Two

The Bible is filled with stories about ordinary men and women who followed God. Many sinned and faltered in their obedience. Those stories bring us hope that God can use normal people today who stumble and fall too. Others in the Bible experienced God's miraculous power. Those stories inspire us when our faith is weak. Most of us like a good story, and the Bible is a glorious story of God and His love for His people.

Not only is the Bible full of stories, but it's also practical teaching for how to live life. It offers guidelines for handling money, dealing with people, managing time, raising children, being a good and godly spouse, and much more.

The Bible also helps us learn how to develop our faith. The Bible teaches us how to pray, how to mature spiritually, and how to obey God when life is tough. God wants to teach us about kingdom living and has filled the Bible with necessary information about that. It's the best place for new Christians to start growing, and it is the place for mature Christians to deepen their faith.

Question Three

According to John, the test of knowledge of God is our moral conduct. It's not how much of the Bible we know, or how much Scripture we can say from memory. The true proof of the knowledge of God is whether or not we obey His commands.

John learned this lesson from Jesus. In the book of Matthew, chapter 25, Jesus taught the disciples about His return. To illustrate, Jesus taught several parables: the parable of the ten virgins, the parable of the talents, and a final parable about the sheep and the goats. It's in the final story that Jesus clearly connected knowing God (and Him knowing us) with obeying His commands.

The parable tells of the Son of Man returning in glory and

gathering all the nations around Him. All people are separated into two groups: sheep and goats. The sheep are on His right, and are those He blesses and invites into His Father's Kingdom. The goats on the left are *"cursed into the eternal fire."* The difference is how they treated those who were hungry, thirsty, naked, sick, or in prison.

The goats try to defend themselves by implying that they would have helped the needy people had they known it was Jesus. *"Lord,"* they say, *"when did we see you hungry or thirsty or a stranger or needing clothes or sick or in prison, and did not help you?"* (Matthew 25:44). Jesus answered, *"I tell you the truth, whatever you did not do for one of the least of these, you did not do for me"* (Matthew 25:45).

When we obey Jesus' commands to care for the poor, to love one another, and to lay down our lives for each other, we show we know God because we are really caring for Jesus.

Question Four

To really know God is to experience the reality of His presence in our lives. Having the reality of God in our lives means doing the things that Jesus did, which means being obedient every day.

True knowledge of God does not end with speculative ideas. It's a similar experience to being trained for a career, such as teaching. You can study in school, learn from books and those who are teaching, but until you prepare a lesson and teach it in front of a class of students, you don't really know teaching. You know about teaching – but you don't know teaching until you've taught.

As Christians, we need both the book knowledge of God and the practical knowledge of knowing God through obeying His commands. We can't obey God's commands unless we know what they are. Then, as we practice obedience in our lives, God's love grows in us. Anyone who has ever experienced a heart transformation from self-focused to others-focused knows the reality of God in his or her life.

Question Five

As we read the Bible—both the Old and the New Testaments—we learn a lot about God's nature. Since God's character does not change (Malachi 3:6), we can learn something about Him from every book of the Bible. It's important to read the entire Bible to know who God really is, not who some people might like Him to be.

In the Old Testament we learn about God's power, love of justice, holiness, and compassion. God describes Himself as a jealous God, desiring complete devotion from His chosen people, the Israelites. In the New Testament, God reveals more of His kindness and the gentleness of a father. All these characteristics show the richness and depth of God's character.

Question Six

We live in a world of "truth decay," which started way back at the beginning of time. In the Garden of Eden, Satan got Eve to question the truth of God's command. Eve knew what God said; it was simple: don't eat from the tree of the knowledge of good and evil or she would die. But Satan asked leading questions, and then denied God's consequences for disobedience, thereby eroding Eve's confidence in the truth. It worked. Eve believed the lies, chose to disobey God and ate the fruit. Since that time, we've been dealing with the effects of that disobedience. Plus, since questioning the truth worked so well on Eve, Satan still uses that tactic on us.

Many people believe it's impossible to really know truth. Because of that, they reason, truth is whatever seems right at the time. Truth for one person isn't truth for another. Truth in this country isn't truth in that country. Nationality, society, history, personality, and emotions can all be the foundation for a person's "truth."

God has a different view of truth—it's found only in Him. Psalm 119:160 says, *"The sum of Thy word is truth, and every one of Thy righteous ordinance is everlasting"* (NASB). When we look to the Bible as the source of truth, we will find answers.

In our society, there are sincere, truth-seeking people who hold contradictory beliefs which both cannot be true, even within the Christian faith. The only way to find the truth on important matters is to seek the Scriptures for answers. God's righteousness is an eternal truth, which shines light on many of today's issues.

Question Seven

An eternal truth is one that has stood the test of time—eternity. Since God is the only being that is eternal (every other being was created), then what God says must be true. If we use a common societal definition for truth, such as, truth is valid for a specific person in a given time and place, then by its very nature, truth will change. How can what is true for me and not you, be eternal? How can anyone believe or stake his life upon that type of "truth"?

On the other hand, we know God said, "I the Lord do not change" (Malachi 3:6). To prove it, the Bible has stood the test of time for thousands of years.

Another difference between eternal truth and a changing truth is that an eternal truth's effect remains the same over time. Sin will always bring about some type of death—spiritual, emotional, or physical. God's love will always bring life. If a dishonest business person invites you to trust him, you can't count on the results of your business deal. If a selfish person promises to love you, you can't depend on her being around for long.

When God's word says something, we can believe it. It's not a fad or someone's opinion, it's eternal truth.

Question Eight

One of the biggest dangers in taking Scripture out of context, or only knowing parts of the Bible, is that we can base our beliefs and decisions on partial truth. It's kind of like taking a multiple-choice test when you are only partly sure of the material. When faced with three answers that sound alike, we realize we really weren't prepared. (See 2 Timothy 4:1-3)

If we aren't completely sure about what God's Word says, then we open ourselves up to compromising the truth. Only knowing bits and pieces of Scripture gives us a limited view of God's plan for our lives and the world. It's like only seeing the trailer and never seeing the full-length movie. When we read and learn all of God's Word, then we are better able to understand the big picture.

Question Nine

A conviction is something you believe so strongly that it determines the way you act. An opinion is something you will argue for, but a conviction is something you'll die for. The people who have made the greatest changes in the world were not the smartest, wealthiest, those with the best upbringing, or the strongest. The greatest changes in our world were made by men and women with the deepest convictions.

Question Ten

It's easy to base our convictions on things other than God's Word. In Bible times and ours, the teachings of Jesus went against many commonly held beliefs. Jesus taught that the first will be last, and that leaders must be servants. Basing our convictions on the Bible is often difficult because it goes against the tide of public opinion.

It's more comfortable to base our convictions on things like our experience, our emotions, or the influence of people we trust and respect. Then, if it gets uncomfortable or challenging to maintain our convictions, we can change them.

Question Eleven

At the end of Hebrews chapter five, the author is imploring the readers to embrace the deeper teachings about righteousness. The readers are Christians who should be advancing in their faith, but instead are still drinking spiritual "milk." Verse 15 states that "solid food," or the deeper teachings of the faith, is for the spiritually mature. The verse also states that ingesting solid food isn't enough – we must train ourselves by constantly using what we are learning in order to distinguish good from evil.

In order to develop biblical convictions, first we must read the Word of God in its entirety. Of course this takes time, but we must start somewhere. Then we study God's Word. We must choose to believe it's true and seek to understand what it says. Being in a Bible study is a great way to do this. Finally, we must meditate on God's Word.

Meditation is simply "chewing" on a portion of God's Word

over and over again. As Christians, we can develop biblical convictions by meditating more on the Bible (see Joshua 1:8).

Questions Twelve

Question 12 requires personal reflection. If some of your members aren't sure why they have some convictions, it might be helpful to discuss this. Also, if some hold convictions that are biblical, encourage them to research the Scriptures so they are better informed about their convictions.

Questions Thirteen and Fourteen

It is not enough to merely read or hear God's Word. We must respond to it by obeying what we read.

Consider how you would feel if you left a note for your daughter asking her to do the dishes while you were at work, but came home to find her watching TV. You'd be pretty frustrated at her disobedience. No parent would be happy because she read the note. The parent wanted her to obey the directions on the note.

If your daughter did the dishes while you were at work, you would be very pleased with her. You would probably thank her -- maybe even with a hug and kiss. Your daughter would experience your pleasure, and feel good about herself for obeying. This is similar to what it's like when we obey what we read in God's Word. We experience our Father's pleasure, and it bolsters our self-confidence and self esteem.

Questions Fifteen and Sixteen

Reading the Bible can be difficult at times. We know it deserves our full attention and that's hard to give at times. Other challenges can be the wording or the historical details. As challenging as reading the Bible can be, the rewards are worth it. If you have time to discuss these questions as a group, share approaches to reading Scripture that have been helpful.

two

Make Prayer a Priority

Questions One and Two

For most of us, parents were our first problem-solvers. If we needed help with homework or cookies for a class treat, we called mom or dad. As we got older, friends become more important. For married couples, a spouse is often the first person to call when there's a flat tire or conflicts with picking up kids. As our children become more independent and capable, they get called to help us, too. Depending on our problem, each of us can quickly identify whom we would call. This can change, however, based on our problem and our friends' areas of expertise, physical ability, and availability.

For each of us, however, there comes a point when we realize we need help that no human can provide. It's in these times of desperation that we call out to God in prayer.

As we read the Bible, we learn that God wants us to pray to Him, asking Him for help with all our problems – both big and small. But more than that, God wants to develop a relationship with us that's only possible through prayer. It's a discipline to go to God in prayer, but there's much God longs to teach us, communicate to us, and do through our prayers.

Question Three

Jesus' listeners would have easily pictured a vineyard as He spoke of vines and branches. A vineyard was a common element of their lives, as they would make wine and raisins from the fruit. The disciples would have envisioned healthy branches, laden with grapes and covered with beautiful green leaves. They also would have known about the bare branches in winter, without fruit but still receiving nutrients from the vine.

Another condition of branches is they must be connected to a healthy vine in order to be healthy themselves. If the vine isn't healthy, if it is not getting nutrients, or if it is diseased, the branches can't be healthy. Conversely, the branches can contract a disease independent of each other, and need to be cut off to keep from affecting the rest of the vine.

Jesus uses this passage to explain a spiritual truth and defines Himself as the vine. Because Jesus is perfect in every way, by staying connected to Him we can remain healthy and fruitful. If we try to get our "food" from any other source, it won't be perfect like Jesus is, and our fruit won't be healthy. It's easy for Christians to seek out help from books or teachers who offer "answers" to life's problems. However, the only true source of strength and nutrition - the only source of life - comes from Jesus.

When we remain or abide in Jesus, we produce healthy fruit. In the Greek language, the word for fruit is *karpos*. It means actual fruit, but it also means our acts or deeds. For a Christian, our "fruit" is our loving and godly deeds. It is evidence of our healthy connection to Jesus if we are acting in a more loving way or choosing more godly deeds.

Question Four

Our connection to Jesus Christ comes from our obedience to the commands of the Bible and prayer. To be an obedient Christian means being aware at all times of how our thoughts and actions line up with, or oppose, the Word of God. This is an everyday responsibility for a Christian. We can't go to church one day a week, then ignore God's commands the other six days.

When we make a decision to obey God's Word, we first have to know God's Word. This involves reading the Bible and applying it to our lives. As we read the Bible, the Holy Spirit helps us understand what God is trying to convey. After we have read and studied the Bible, we have to choose to obey. This process of learning and application of Scripture turns our minds to the things of God more and more. As we do this, we are abiding in Christ.

The other key to abiding in Jesus Christ is prayer. When we come to God in prayer, humbly confessing any known sin and seeking to know God more, we experience God in an intimate way. Just as the branch needs the vine for its very survival, we need God. When we acknowledge that need in prayer, we are dedicating ourselves to "remain" or "abide" in Him.

Question Five

One of the biggest misconceptions for any Christian is that he or she is able to handle life's problems alone. This creates a problem in prayer because we don't feel a dependence upon, or need for, God. We think we can do it ourselves. Ever since Adam and Eve, man has vastly overestimated his ability. Even in the Garden of Eden, Adam and Eve thought they knew better than God and disobeyed Him by eating from the forbidden tree. They took matters into their own hands, and we have paid the penalty for that overconfidence (a.k.a., sin) since that time.

We go through life thinking, "I don't need to pray about that, because it's something I can do on my own!" To become an effective Christian , we must admit we need God's help with everything.

It's not that we can't accomplish a task without Jesus. People go around living busy lives, getting lots done. But taken within the context of this teaching of Jesus, we can't produce any truly healthy spiritual fruit without Him. It may look like a healthy grape, but it's not healthy on the inside without Jesus as the vine.

Question Six

When we don't see our need for God, then prayer becomes a religious duty. The basic motivation behind this is guilt. We think, "I know I should pray more, I ought to pray more. It's something I need to do!" It's almost like there's a sense of obligation, because if we don't pray, we'll be on God's "bad list." As a result, it's easy to go through a meaningless ritual that becomes a rut.

If we see our need for God only in the "big" areas of life, then we can consider prayer like a first aid kit – only to be used in case of emergency. For some, prayer is a last act of desperation. We try every resource available and, if all else fails, we pray. This type of prayer can happen when we don't think God cares about the details of our lives, or it can develop when we have pride in our lives. Both attitudes can hinder the growth of our relationship with God through prayer.

Question Seven

The first direction is to not be anxious about anything. The word "anxious" conveys self-centered worry and fretfulness. This passage isn't saying we aren't to care about things. As Christians, we are to have sincere and legitimate care for many things. But we aren't to be anxious or worried. Anxiety also contains a component of impatience. We want a resolution to our problem, and we want it now!

For most of us, not being anxious is easier said than done. God knows this and included the next part of the Scripture with specific instructions on what to do. When we have a request, we are to present it to God through prayer and petition. For some, this comes naturally. It's easy to present a list of concerns to God. For others, this is a challenge. It seems like we are "bothering" God with our petty problems. This will take a choice on our part to overcome that concern. It might be helpful to write out your requests in order to pray more effectively. Then you can keep track of how God answers your prayers, and you will have more about which to praise Him.

As the teaching note in the study said, these two words, prayer and petition, have slightly different meanings. The first involves a more worshipful attitude and the second is to request something. This might sound like we are buttering God up by telling Him how wonderful He is, then asking for something. But with the right heart, it's a graceful flow. We worship and adore God first in prayer, and then we are more aware of how able He is to answer our requests.

Finally, we are to have a thankful heart when we pray. Everyone, no matter how dire his or her circumstance, has something to be thankful for. Thankfulness can include specifically thanking God for the good things He gives us, but it's also a general attitude. We've all known people who have a critical attitude, and easily identify the bad in a given situation. On the other hand, we've met people with a grateful attitude that permeates every interaction. Thankfulness is a choice we make to see God's goodness and blessings every day.

Question Eight

Paul, the author of Philippians, addresses this question by inviting us to present all of our requests to God. The Scripture says "in everything," which means today, what it meant then: everything. This means that God cares about addressing even the smallest of your concerns.

Prayer is the way we make our requests known to God, and it's His chosen method of meeting our needs. In fact, the Bible teaches that there are some things that God has promised to do for us only if we pray and ask! Some people think, "God knows what I need, so I don't need to ask Him." However, God has set up in His plan that we need to ask for some things. James 4:2c says, "You do not have because you do not ask" (NASB). Over 20 times in the New Testament the Bible says, "Ask!" This is a command, not a suggestion.

Question Nine

When we are worried and anxious, we have effectively placed our faith in something other than God. I (Glynnis) struggle with worry in a few areas of my life—one of which is flying. After suffering through some white-knuckled flights, I realized I was anxious because I had placed my faith in the pilot, the weather, and the mechanic who checked the engine of the plane. I should have placed my faith in God, who is the only one who can truly protect me. Worry and anxiety were a symptom of my misplaced faith. When I acknowledged this lack of faith, confessed it to God, and presented my request for safety with thanksgiving, I experienced the miraculous peace that Scripture talks about.

Worry turns our dependence from God onto ourselves or someone else. It weakens our faith that God actually cares, and can do something about our problem. If worry keeps us from praying, then we are missing out on the unlimited power and resources that God has to offer.

Question Eleven

One of the most exciting things about prayer is that it's an act of cooperation. God has sovereignly chosen for us to cooperate with Him by praying, and helping see His will done on earth. In this passage, Jesus gives His disciples an amazing, almost unbelievable, promise: they will do the works He did—and greater works.

Imagine that! Jesus raised the dead and fed 5,000 men with five loaves and two fishes. Did He really mean His disciples would do something like that? This passage makes it clear that we are to be following in the footsteps of Jesus, using Him as our model for how to live out the Kingdom of God here on earth. Using Jesus as our guide, we get an exciting picture of how life should, and could, be.

As we look through the Gospels, we read about many of the works and miracles Jesus did. Use the stories of Jesus' life to learn more about what we should be doing today.

Question Twelve

Prayer is the key to this happening in our lives. In verse 13, Jesus said, "And I will do whatever you ask in my name, so that the Son may bring glory to the Father." Jesus' plan was to multiply His ministry after His departure. He didn't want the church to fall apart, but grow and continue to impact the world. He gave His disciples a personal guarantee—ask in His Name and He will answer.

Jesus' promise to answer our prayers comes with a condition: that God is glorified. This means that we need to be praying for God's will, and seeking to bring glory and honor to Him in what we ask. Sometimes we pray and ask for something selfish and expect God to answer "yes." Jesus was clearly saying that the disciples were to pray in order to continue His work on earth.

Questions Thirteen and Fourteen

Depending on the comfort level between the members of your group, consider sharing these personal answers. These questions can be a springboard for your group to start praying for each other, or to expand on your prayer ministry within the group. Consider keeping a group prayer journal of your requests and God's answers, then spend time praising God and thanking Him together.

Imagine being a parent and not having your children talk to you. This must be how God feels when we don't pray. Prayer is an important topic to address because it's our daily method of communicating with God, our Creator, our Savior, our Heavenly Father, and our friend. Imagine what God might want to do if all His children prayed like Jesus!

three

Living a Life of Obedience

Question One

Disobedience comes naturally to most of us. That's one thing we don't need to teach kids how to do! Unless obedience is taught early, using healthy and appropriate consequences, many people go through life thinking that breaking rules is OK as long as they aren't caught. Or, they think breaking rules is OK because everyone else is doing it. This applies to everything from traffic laws, to how we use our time at work, to "fudging" on our income taxes.

This first question is designed to get the participant thinking about how a child disobeys a parent. For most of us, this is our first experience in disobedience. How a child thinks and why he disobeys, isn't too different from adults.

As Christians, we have "rules" to obey that others don't because our Heavenly Father has asked us to do (and not do) certain things. Disobedience is a heart issue and one goal of this study is to examine why we choose to disobey.

Question Two

Making choices that deviate from God's Word will always lead someone away from God's best for his or her life. Being obedient to God consists of a sequence of right choices every day. One main difference between successful people and those who never live up to their potential is that successful people choose to do the things that most people are unwilling to do. For Christians, this means choosing to obey God in the small and large things.

Question Three

Jesus tells the parable of the talents in the middle of three stories about what it will be like at the end of the age, when Christ returns. The first parable is about ten virgins who fell asleep while waiting for their bridegroom. The third parable is about a King who will separate people based on whether or not they cared for the most vulnerable members of society. Sandwiched between these stories is the parable of the talents. The point of this parable is to be ready when Christ returns by being obedient and a good steward of all that God has entrusted to us now.

In the time this parable was told, servants or slaves were given great amounts of responsibility, much more than slaves of recent history. In fact, many slaves were almost considered partners in their master's venture. This parable illustrates such a relationship. Not only were the slaves allowed to make decisions on their own, but they were entrusted with a great responsibility.

Matthew 25:14 says the master entrusted his property to three of his servants in the form of a "talent." The "talent" mentioned in the parable was a unit of exchange. Estimates of its value vary. The value of the talent isn't critical to the point of the story. What is most important is what the servants did with their responsibilities.

At least two of the servants knew the master's wishes when they received the talents. Verse 16 says "The man who had received the five talents went at once and put his money to work …" Likewise, the second man did the same "at once." The master was expecting them to handle the talents like he would, and that was to invest it in order to make a profit.

Another interesting element to the parable is that each servant was given a different amount in the first place "according to his ability." This indicates it wasn't an arbitrary decision on the part of the master. The master must have known which servant would be more responsible and fulfill the task assigned.

Question Four

When the master returned from his trip, the servants came to his home to settle accounts. Each one had an opportunity to present his results to the master. The parable tells us what the master expected them to do and that was to be "faithful with a few things." The master didn't set a goal for each servant, nor were there quotas; he simply wanted their obedience and faithfulness.

Question Five

The master is very pleased with the first and second servants who doubled their talents. Not only does he verbally express his pleasure by calling them "good and faithful" servants, but he offers a promise of two rewards. The first is to be put in charge of many things, and the second is to share in the master's happiness.

The third servant, however, receives a much different response. The final servant didn't fulfill his master's expectations. Instead of wisely handling the talent, he dug a hole in the ground and hid the master's money. The master severely corrected him, calling him a "wicked, lazy servant." Not only did he earn the displeasure of his master, but the third servant got his one talent taken away and was sent away from the comfort of his home.

The master's expectation is very simple: obedience. The master needs to trust that his servants will do what they are told while he is away. The application for us is the same. God needs to trust that we will do what He asks us to do. He's looking for faithful men and women to depend upon. (see 2 Chronicles16:9)

Question Six

The third servant had a ready excuse for not obeying his master. It's actually the master's fault, according to the servant. He started by trying to shift the blame for his error to the master, calling him a hard man and one who takes advantage of the work of others. He claimed his fear made him disobedient.

It's possible that the third servant was annoyed at receiving one talent while his co-workers were given more. His bitterness and resentment could have led him down the path of disobedience.

Question Seven

The third servant might have looked at the one talent he had been given and thought, "It's only one talent. It's no big deal! Everyone's got at least one talent." This attitude would diminish the importance of his master's request.

Sometimes we might look at the responsibilities God has given us and think similarly. Perhaps we look at caring for our homes as a "one talent" responsibility, and neglect its upkeep. Maybe being a parent seems like an "ordinary job," so we diminish its importance. Or, we "only" serve in the nursery at church, which seems like a job of little worth; so we stroll in late or call in sick at the last minute. It's easy, but dangerous, to devalue those "jobs" God assigns when they seem insignificant compared to bigger and better opportunities.

Question Eight

Jesus tells this straightforward story to the chief priest and elders. They had been questioning Jesus' authority to do the things He did. Jesus knew they were trying to trick Him, and refused to answer their questions. He did, however, tell this story of the man with two sons.

In this parable, Jesus is rebuking the Jewish leaders who claimed to love God but didn't follow God's will. Jesus very boldly tells them that the tax collectors and the prostitutes get it! Even though they lived lives far from God, they are repenting and turning to God. The religious leaders, on the other hand, mouth their obedience to God, then ignore His commands. It's not enough to say we will obey God, we actually have to do it.

Question Nine

The second son could have disobeyed his father for a number of reasons. Jesus doesn't list any of them. The son's ready "yes" indicates a bold-faced lie, or only a surface desire to obey his father. Perhaps the son never really meant to go work in the vineyard. If that's the case, then he added lying and pride to his offenses against his father.

Two other options are that something better came along, or the work seemed too hard and the second son changed his mind. Both of these responses reveal a weak character and lack of commitment to integrity. Being trustworthy is of high importance to God. Jesus said, "Simply let your 'Yes' be 'Yes,' and your 'No,' 'No'; anything beyond this comes from the evil one" (Matthew 5:37).

Questions Ten and Eleven

When we commit to living for Jesus, the Holy Spirit comes to empower us to fulfill that commitment. From that time on, Christians will receive promptings to do certain things. Plus, as we read the Bible and learn the truth, God speaks to us about things through His Word. Then, as we mature in our faith, from time to time, God will ask us to do something. It could be to invite a neighbor to church, share our faith with a family member, or start to tithe. We "know" we are supposed to do it, but we push it to the bottom of our "to do" list, or we rationalize that it wasn't God, just a guilty conscience. When God wants us to obey, He's got a gentle way of bringing His request in front of us.

These two questions will allow each participant to get honest with God about his obedience or lack of it. As you prepare for your study, pray for God to speak to each member of your group, and for hearts to be ready to hear.

Question Twelve

With this story, Jesus is saying, "better late than never." Although we tend to think of delayed obedience as disobedience, Jesus extends an invitation to repent and obey no matter what we've done. Jesus is also saying that we can't earn righteousness based on what we do. Righteousness only comes through faith in Jesus Christ.

Questions Thirteen and Fourteen

Loving Jesus and obeying Jesus cannot be separated. Jesus knows anyone can say they love Him, but keeping his commands actually shows that love.

Our obedience also shows that Jesus Christ is Lord of our lives, and that we trust Him. Many times we won't understand why Jesus is asking us to do something – it won't seem right to our human minds. We wonder, how can forgiving our enemies be right? or, why should we put ourselves at risk to help someone we don't know? These are times when our obedience is a declaration of our faith. After all God has done for us, obedience is a small price to pay to show our gratitude and love.

Questions Fifteen and Sixteen

These questions are very personal in nature. They should lead the participant to evaluate his or her own level of obedience. We all have parts of our lives and hearts that we hold back from God. Living a life of obedience is a process that takes one step at a time.

Your small group can be a great source of support to help members deal with areas of disobedience. As your members share personal struggles, make a commitment to pray for each other. It might help to offer accountability for each other. Pray about how you might best do that. If you pair up, be sure to match females together and males together.

Questions Seventeen and Eighteen

These verses in Romans chapter 6, come on the heels of a discussion about sin and grace. The Jewish people had been under the Mosaic law for so many years that they had to learn what it meant to be under grace. They knew how to atone for sin under the law—that meant a sacrifice. But they were learning how to address sin under the new "law" of grace.

Paul is addressing a fact familiar to his listeners, and to us: whatever we submit ourselves to becomes our master. When we commit sin, we are slaves to sin. However, when we choose the righteous life in Jesus, we are slaves to obedience. Our reward for being a slave to obedience is freedom from bondage to sin, which separates us from God.

Another reward of obedience is a simple, honest life. When we obey God's commands, there's no need to cover our tracks or remember who we lied to. Our life is uncomplicated because we don't have to pretend we are something we are not.

Questions Nineteen and Twenty

Because of our sin nature, obedience doesn't come naturally. Our natural focus is to choose our way rather than God's way. However, obedience is possible with the help of the Holy Spirit. In our own understanding, our ways seems right, but scripture is clear where that lead us. (see Proverbs 14:12)

Obedience leads to life, and it starts with saying one small "yes" after another.

four

Give to God

Questions One and Two

We have all spent money on things we regret. We try and save money on a cheaper brand and it ends up breaking. Or, we spend too much money on an item and find it on sale the next week. Another source of regret when spending money is hoping something will bring us satisfaction, only to find that it doesn't.

Hopefully, these questions will ease discomfort regarding talking about money. Almost everybody has similar experiences with money. We've made foolish investments, borrowed it unwisely, spent it carelessly, and wondered where it went at the end of the month. The good news is we can always start fresh with our money management. This lesson covers the best place to start, and that's returning a portion of our income to God.

Question Three

The prophet Malachi starts this passage by addressing the faithfulness of God in not destroying His chosen people when they turned away. This promise was given to Noah after God destroyed the inhabitants of the earth in a flood, saving only Noah and his family. Genesis 8:21 says, "The Lord smelled the pleasing aroma and said in his heart: 'Never again will I curse the ground because of man, even though every inclination of his heart is evil from childhood. And never again will I destroy all living creatures, as I have done.'"

In spite of the waywardness of God's chosen people for generations, He loved them still. Although God is faithful, He is still a holy God, calling for obedience and devotion. This passage shows God's displeasure with how they disobeyed by not keeping His decrees and turning away from Him to seek other gods or to please themselves.

The second way the Israelites disobeyed God was by not bringing the whole tithe into the storehouse. Malachi bluntly proclaims the Israelites' sin with a question: "Will a man rob God?" The first way many of us think of robbing a person is to take something from them. In this instance, the people were stealing from God by keeping what was His to begin with. It's sort of like borrowing a lawnmower from a neighbor and then only returning the grass catcher. Your neighbor gave you the lawnmower to use and expected the entire machine to be returned. God has given us everything we have, and asks for 10% of our income in return. To be obedient, we need to carefully assess all areas of income, and return to God a tithe of all of it.

Question Four

God's first desire is that our hearts are right with Him. He calls us to a life of devotion to Him and to advance His Kingdom here on earth. God could ask for half of what we have to test our devotion and obedience, but instead only asks for ten percent.

Question Five

It is shown throughout scripture that the tithes were used to support those who worked in ministry. In the Old Testament, the family of Levi, the Levites, were set apart from the rest of the Israelites and assigned the care of the temple (the house of God). The Levites serves as priests, cared for the sacred parts of the temple, and took care of all the minor details of maintaining the house of the Lord. They were given no land for themselves and no way to produce income. Because of this, the Levites were provided for by the tithes of the Israelites.

The tradition of caring for those "employed" by the church continued in the New Testament. In 1 Corinthians 9:13 Paul records, "Don't you know that those who work in the temple get their food from the temple, and those who serve at the altar share in what is offered on the altar? In the same way, the Lord has commanded that those who preach the gospel should receive their living from the gospel."

The New Testament church was also designed to be a place of ministry for those in need. The church wasn't necessarily a building as we think of it today. Instead it was a group of people. We read in Acts of the church caring for the spiritual and practical needs of the congregation. Acts 2:44-45 reads, "All the believers were together and had everything in common. Selling their possessions and goods, they gave to anyone as he had need." Giving our tithe to the local church helps assure this care continues.

Question Six

God promises abundant blessings when we obey Him with our financial resources. Over and over the Bible promises that giving sets in motion a series of divine blessings in our lives. Not only financial blessings, but also spiritual, relational, material, emotional, physical, and social.

In Malachi 3:10b, God says, "'Test me in this,' says the Lord Almighty, 'and see if I will not throw open the floodgates of heaven and pour out so much blessing that you will not have room enough for it.'" In this same passage, God promises to protect them from destruction to their crops so they can continue to return ten percent in the future.

Other passages where we find promises of blessings include Luke 6:38, "Give, and it will be given to you. They will pour into your lap a good measure – pressed down, shaken together, and running over" (NASB). Proverbs 3:9-10 holds a promise as well, "Honor the Lord from your wealth and from the first of all your produce; so your barns will be filled with plenty and your vats will overflow with new wine" (NASB).

Question Seven

Obedience is at the core of being a Christian. Jesus' last instructions to His disciples involved teaching others to obey: "Therefore go and make disciples of all nations, baptizing them in the name of the Father and of the Son and of the Holy Spirit, and teaching them to obey everything I have commanded you. And surely I am with you always, to the very end of the age" (Matthew 28:19).

We show that God is first in our lives by obeying His commands. We obey the small ones that seem incidental, and we obey the difficult ones that take constant prayer and encouragement from our brothers and sisters in Christ.

Every moment of the day brings opportunities to put God first by obeying His commands. Your group can take a typical day and walk through it, identifying opportunities to put God first—including getting ready for the day, driving to work or school, interacting with a friend, and stopping at the store in the evening. We put God first every time we choose to act according to His commandments and not our own desires.

Question Eight

Money, and the things it can buy, has great potential to become our master. Jesus acknowledged this potential in His teachings. In Matthew 6:24, Jesus said, "No one can serve two masters. Either he will hate the one and love the other, or he will be devoted to the one and despise the other. You cannot serve both God and Money."

Money takes first place every time we choose to withhold ten percent of our income from God. It takes first place every time we spend it on our "wants" instead of others' or our "needs." When we get into debt, money can control our decisions. When we choose a job for money, instead of asking God where He wants us to work, money takes first place.

Question Nine

Money is a great equalizer. We all use it and have opportunities to serve God with it. We don't all have the same amount of money, but that doesn't seem to matter as much as our obedience and heart attitude about giving.

There's a beautiful vignette in the New Testament, when Jesus observed a poor widow at the offering plate (see Mark 12:41-44). We don't all have the same physical skills, or spiritual gifts, or intellectual ability. But every person, even the poorest widow, has an opportunity to put God first with his or her money.

Question Ten

This teaching by Jesus specifically mentions a treasure that moth or rust could destroy. Our first thoughts would lead us to think of clothing or items made of metal. We might also think Jesus is talking about the furniture inside our homes.

But, was Jesus really meaning things like cloth and metal? Perhaps. It's more likely that Jesus was talking about anything on this earth that we purchase for selfish reasons. With that outlook, a house or a car could fall into either category. If we purchase a big house for status, then it's an earthly treasure. If we purchase a big home to provide hospitality for missionaries on furlough or unwed mothers, then it might fall into the heavenly treasure category. The house isn't the actual treasure, but the deeds of hospitality and love accomplished through the house can never rust or deteriorate.

Likewise, we could donate money to the church and make sure everyone knows about it. Although the money would be used for God's purposes, it might not be credited to our heavenly account because our motive was self-centered.

Question Eleven

A heavenly treasure here on earth would be something that has good and eternal significance. Since there are only two things on this earth that will last eternally—God's Word and people—those are the "treasures" we should seek. What we do for and with people and the Bible will have eternal value.

Examples of this might be loving and kind deeds, sacrificing something for Christ's sake, forgiving someone, giving of our time and finances to advance the Kingdom, time spent studying the Bible, encouraging someone in prison, or clothing and feeding the homeless and downtrodden. The opportunities for investing in heavenly treasures are unlimited.

Question Twelve

When we start seeing people as eternal beings, our perspective changes. When we consider that God's Word has eternal impact, we should read it with hunger, devouring every word. No longer is there room for casual interaction with either people or God's Word.

What we do for other people would fall into the heavenly treasure category because we are commanded to love others. In Matthew chapter 22 the Pharisees asked Jesus about the greatest commandment. Jesus replied, "Love the Lord your God with all your heart and with all your soul and with all your mind. This is the first and greatest commandment. And the second is like it: Love your neighbor as yourself. All the Law and the Prophets hang on these two commandments."

Isn't it interesting that the Pharisees didn't ask Jesus to identify the second greatest commandment? Jesus volunteered that information because it is intertwined with the first. It's not enough to love God; we also have to love others. People will live eternally somewhere. God loves people so much that He wants them to spend eternity with Him.

When we invest in things of eternal significance, it also changes our attitude towards God. As we participate in His work on earth, we start to see things from His perspective. This expands our understanding of God and offers us increasing reasons to praise Him and seek to honor Him with our actions.

Questions Thirteen and Fourteen

Unfortunately, statistics show that most Christians in the United States only give about two to three percent of their income back to God. Imagine what could happen to advance the Kingdom if Christians gave ten percent. Imagine how much we could do with that money and how God might bless our communities and nation.

This is a hard lesson, but it is a critical one to becoming an effective Christian. As the leader, please pray that God will move the hearts of your group to start giving according to His Word.

five

LIVE IN COMMUNITY

Questions One and Two

The bottom line about community is that we need each other. In the story of creation found in Genesis, there was only one thing God proclaimed "not good." That was for man to be alone. From the very beginning we were designed for community.

Loneliness is one of the worst feelings we can experience. That's why good Christian friends are one of God's greatest gifts to His creation. The right friends can build us up. Conversely, the wrong friends can bring us down.

The first questions in this study invite the participant to think about the positives of having friends and being in a community. Being in a community of loving friends offers a multitude of benefits that this study will only touch upon. Of course, there are always challenges when people get together, but with God as our foundation, we can overcome hurdles and develop relationships that change us for the better and enrich our lives beyond measure.

Question Three

There is great power in the words and presence of someone who loves us. Have you ever gone through a difficult time and called someone you love just to hear his or her voice? Or, have you ever walked into church and sought out a friend to get a much-needed hug or pat on the back? (see Ecclesiastes 4:9-11)

When we are part of a community, we get to know each other—we learn each other's strengths and weaknesses. We can speak words of affirmation about each other's strengths. Plus, we can speak loving words that build up the weak spots.

Ephesians 4:14-16 gives us insight into how a community can encourage us. This passage follows on the heels of Paul's appeal to develop unity in the church. According to this passage in Ephesians, after we reach a level of godly unity, this will happen:

"Then we will no longer be infants, tossed back and forth by the waves, and blown here and there by every wind of teaching and by the cunning and craftiness of men in their deceitful scheming. Instead, speaking the truth in love, we will in all things grow up into him who is the Head, that is, Christ. From him the whole body, joined and held together by every supporting ligament, grows and builds itself up in love, as each part does its work."

This passage shows us that through community we can stand firm on the truth and, consequently, won't be influenced by deceitful men. Also, we will speak the truth in love to each other. When we know someone loves us, it's much easier to take correction. We also learn that we will encourage each other to become more like Jesus.

Question Four

God doesn't want church, or a small group, to be something you just go to. There's a big difference between attending a church service and being a part of the community. God wants church to be a family of which you are an active part.

Ephesians 2:19 says, "So then you are no longer strangers and aliens, but you are fellow citizens with the saints, and are of God's household, ..." (NASB). God is saying being a Christian doesn't mean just believing. It means belonging.

When we belong to something, we take better care of it. In a healthy Christian community, the members care for each other in all aspects of their lives. This includes spiritual, emotional, relational, and practical matters.

From a practical standpoint, just a few attributes of a healthy community include a commitment to meet together on a regular basis, a commitment to honesty, speaking words in kindness and love, thinking the best of others, and putting the needs of others before our own.

Question Five

Two of the best ways to spur one another on to good deeds are honesty and accountability. This starts with being honest about our challenges. Then, having others pray for us and ask us about our progress spurs us on.

I (Brian) have been part of some sort of small group, living in community with other people, almost the entire time I've been a Christian. During that time, I've confided in different people about areas I was struggling in at that particular time. It could have been a problem at work when I was a teacher. Or it might have been some sort of financial problem. Whenever I confided in people, they would almost always follow up with me later and say, "How's it been going in that particular area?" If I hadn't done anything to address the issue, they just continued to pray for me. Then, the next time they saw me, they asked the same question, "How's it been going in that particular area?" Pretty soon I figured out that I was going to have to take some action on that issue. Otherwise, they would just keep asking me the same question.

Here's the truth, we all need someone to keep asking us those types of questions. Without community, we can easily drift away from doing the things we know are right and good.

Question Six

Jesus speaks of the importance of meeting in His name. We can go to lots of meetings throughout the day—work meetings, parent meetings for sports teams, PTA meetings, and Scouts meetings, to list a few. What a difference when we gather in the name of Jesus!

The Greek translation for the word "name" has a few meanings. One of them is "the cause or reason named." When we gather in the name of Jesus, we are taking up His cause, we are gathering for a reason—Him! We are proclaiming that we will follow where Jesus leads and declaring our allegiance to Him..

Question Seven

Imagine setting up the backyard barbeque and using charcoal briquettes. You have to pile the briquettes against each other for the fire to spread and to create enough heat to cook your food. If you take one of the briquettes away and put it off to the side by itself, it cools off fast. It will lose its heat and not fulfill its function.

When the briquettes stick together, then there is heat and they feed off each other. That's the way it is with Christians, too. Dallas

Willard said it this way, "Personalities united can contain more of God, and sustain the force of His presence, much better than scattered individuals."

Question Eight

Let's use a knife or blade for an example to answer this question. A knife or a blade is typically used to cut something such as meat, vegetables, cloth, or wood. As it is used, it becomes dull. There can be little chips that develop in the edge of the blade. Cutting will render the blade ineffective, and on its own, it will never become sharp again.

When a blade is dull, it's much harder to use. Not only does it take more force to actually cut something, but it is also harder to control. That's why chefs keep their knives sharpened. A dull blade is actually more dangerous than a sharp one.

When a blade is sharpened, it is done for a purpose. It's not so the knife can look better. Sharpening is done to make it more effective and efficient. A knife is sharpened so that it can actually do something. If we sharpen a knife for years and never put it into use, it will eventually be sharpened down to nothing.

Turning this into a spiritual application, we are to be sharpened and sharpen others in order to advance the Kingdom of God. Sharpening iron isn't a passive activity, but a battle, and Christians are in a spiritual battle all the time (Ephesians 6:10-13).

Author Tony Woodlief writes: "It seems to me that too many of us—and I am at the top of this list—spend our precious free time diligently sharpening, sharpening, sharpening, and we never look up from our grindstones to ask where the battle is."

Question Nine

The first truth about sharpening iron is that a knife cannot sharpen itself. Nor can something weaker than iron sharpen iron. In order for a Christian to be sharpened, that person must be around other people who are spiritually mature.

A godly Christian friend will sharpen you in areas they are strong. For example, a wise friend will make you wiser. A loving friend will expand your capacity to love. A biblically knowledgeable friend will enhance your understanding of scripture. Proverbs 13:20 says, "He who walks with the wise grows wise, but a companion of fools suffers harm."

We are also called to exhort, warn, and correct each other at times. First Thessalonians 5:14 says, "And we urge you, brothers, warn those who are idle, encourage the timid, help the weak, be patient with everyone." Galatians 6:1-2 says, "Brothers, if someone is caught in a sin, you who are spiritual should restore him gently. But watch yourself, or you also may be tempted. Carry each other's burdens, and in this way you will fulfill the law of Christ."

Question Ten

In the story of creation, found in the book of Genesis, Adam and Eve at first wore no clothing. God created them "naked, and they felt no shame" (Genesis 2:25). Adam and Eve had a perfect, unblemished relationship with each other and with God. There were no secrets; there was no hiding – just honesty.

That all changed the moment Adam and Eve sinned. As soon as they ate the fruit, the Bible says, " ... the eyes of both of them were opened, and they realized they were naked; so they sewed fig leaves together and made coverings for themselves" (Genesis 3:7). Then, as if He couldn't find them, they hid from God among the trees.

What a dramatic change from just moments before. One minute they were in perfect harmony with each other and God—the next they are covering themselves from each other and hiding from God. Scripture says Adam and Eve hid because they were afraid due to their nakedness (Genesis 3:10).

Since that time, the human race has been afraid of exposing our sin and weaknesses. We've been in hiding ever since, and the church is no exception. Some hide by not even going to church, in order to not be exposed to others. But some hide inside the church by putting on a happy face and pretending all is OK.

Not only did Adam and Eve sever their perfect unity with each other and God, but they also resorted to finger-pointing and blame to cover their sin. Eve blamed the serpent, and Adam blamed Eve and God: "The man said, 'The woman you put here with me—she gave me some fruit from the tree, and I ate it'"(Genesis 3:12).

Adam and Eve's disobedience stemmed from pride—they wanted to be like God. That was Satan's downfall and he knew it would work on God's creation. Pride is often the reason we aren't willing to be open with each other. We want to pretend we are something we aren't, and as a result hide our true selves from the world.

Question Eleven

Many of the healing miracles Jesus performed involved physical healings. But Jesus also healed broken hearts, broken relationships, broken dreams, and broken identities. These are just some of the types of healing we can experience when we confess our sins to each other and pray for each other.

Community is the one place where it is fully safe for us to take off our masks and know the healing power of being known and loved. Before Adam and Eve sinned, they were naked and not ashamed. The idea behind this is there were no secrets. They were fully known and loved. Everything about them was revealed.

What happens in many churches is that people attend every week, but no one knows them, and they are dying inside. Nobody knows their fears, their dreams, or their problems. That's not Jesus' plan for His community. The only way to receive healing is to make the choice to begin living in community with other people.

Questions Thirteen and Fourteen

The opportunity for growth through being a member of a Christian community is open to everyone. But it's our responsibility to become an active part of the community. We can't attend church and expect others to meet all our needs. It's in serving others that we fulfill God's design for the church.

SIX

SERVE OTHERS

Questions One and Two

We live in a service industry dominated culture. Somewhere there is someone willing to do what we don't want to do. Whether it's wash our cars, paint our toenails, or manage our money, someone is willing to perform a service and others are willing to receive a service—for a price. Christian service, however, is supposed to be done differently. We are all to be serving with no expectation of payment. Talk about a paradigm shift in thinking. These questions will prepare the participants to think about God's attitude toward serving.

Question Three

Before we were even born, God planned a life of service for each of us. He planned good works for us to do. This is one reason so many people are miserable today. It's the reason they feel empty, without significance or purpose. If we aren't fulfilling our God-given design to serve others, we are missing one of the great purposes of our lives.

Jesus modeled serving others and taught about the importance of service during His entire time of ministry here on earth. Jesus taught this lesson to His disciples when two of them asked for places of honor in heaven. Jesus said, "… whoever wants to become great among you must be your servant, and whoever wants to be first must be your slave—just as the Son of Man did not come to be served, but to serve, and to give his life as a ransom for many" (Matthew 20:26-28).

Jesus particularly modeled service to the outcasts of society. He willingly sought out people suffering with illness, disease, and demon possession. He touched and healed the lepers, who were shunned from society. He cared for servants and children, the lowest social rank. He taught women, and treated them as equals, when most of society did not value women. Jesus showed kindness to the tax collectors, who were despised for their selfish interests. He honored those who would bring even a cup of cold water to someone in His name.

Over and over, Jesus performed deeds of kindness and acts of service to everyone He met. While we may not have the exact same types of social outcasts and oppressed people, there are many who would fall into similar categories. Who are these people? Perhaps they are drug addicts, thieves in prison, or AIDS orphans in Africa. For most of us, the type of service Jesus modeled will put us outside our comfort zone.

However, that's not the only type of service Jesus modeled. Jesus honored His parents, taught others, led a small group, cared for His friends, and many other commonplace acts of service. Jesus showed us that God values every act of service we do.

Question Four

This question is one that is an important one for us to explore in greater depth. The easiest place to start figuring out where we are to serve is to identify some of our natural gifts and talents. Consider God as a master painter. He has colored your life in very unique ways:

- your personality
- your likes and dislikes
- your talents
- your physical ability
- your learning style
- your social interaction style
- your spiritual gifts

Some people can easily identify their natural talents. They may quickly list things like teaching or athletics. Others may need to think about this. If their level of self-esteem is low, this may be difficult. They may believe they have no abilities God could use. This is a lie and tool of Satan to take us out of God's service. It will take God's truth to counteract this lie. The truth is found in God's Word about our worth and God's intentional design for our lives:

> "For you created my inmost being; you knit me together in my mother's womb. I praise you because I am fearfully and wonderfully made; your works are wonderful, I know that full well."
>
> — Psalm 139:13-14

If this is a challenging question for some, perhaps the group can spend some time helping those people identify some of their natural gifts and talents. This is an important step in helping some Christians get off the bench and into the game.

Question Five

This passage first tells us that Jesus came to give Himself for us in order to redeem us from all wickedness. We were all lost in sin before we met Jesus. Believing in Jesus redeems us, or pays the price, for our sin. But it doesn't stop there, although many Christians are content with their redemption. Jesus redeemed us to do good works with an eager heart.

Question Six

When we become a Christian, our old nature dies, and we become a new creation. This doesn't always happen overnight, but it is happening a little bit every day. In our old nature, we were self-focused. Serving would be done with the intent to get something for ourselves. However, with our new nature, we have the ability to think more like Jesus, and we also receive the gift of the Holy Spirit. It's only with the Holy Spirit that we can think beyond ourselves and be eager to do what is good with no thought of reward.

Question Seven

This passage is saying that one of the ways we prove we belong to Christ is by being zealous, or eager, to do good deeds. Good deeds are proof that we belong to Christ because it's God's design for His church. In the New Testament we find several references to the church being the body of Christ, with each person having a specific responsibility. First Corinthians 12:27 says, "Now you are the body of Christ, and each one of you is a part of it." Then in

Ephesians, we read that we are called to service to build up the body of Christ. (See Ephesians 4:11-13.)

God's design for the church was that we would be serving each other for a purpose, and that purpose is to build each other up, and build up the church. If we are not serving, then we are not doing our part of helping ourselves and others reach unity and increase in our knowledge of Jesus.

Question Eight

Paul is giving instructions for holy living in the third chapter of Colossians. In this passage, Paul is specifically speaking to slaves. Paul isn't condoning slavery here; he's giving instructions on how to live right in the midst of very difficult conditions. Paul is calling for individuals to set their minds above their circumstances when serving others. This isn't to be a temporary mind-set, but a permanent change in the way we think about serving.

When we consider our service being for Jesus, it dignifies even the most menial task. When a mother changes the tenth diaper of the day, or a volunteer empties trash cans in the church office, their work has great meaning. To consider every act of service as serving Jesus turns our mind towards the eternal impact of our service, rather than the mundane, day-to-day grind.

Question Nine

One reason serving is often difficult is because it's counterintuitive to what we've learned all our lives. In the world, you build a pyramid and climb to the top. It's kind of a "dog-eat-dog" way of thinking. You win by intimidation. You look out for number one and step on others as you climb to the top.

Jesus said the exact opposite of what the world says about how to live life. Jesus' definition of the Christian life included setting aside our pride to serve others in the areas of their greatest need. Most people like to serve God; they just aren't too excited about serving others.

Some types of service are difficult because we have to overcome beliefs we may have held for years. We may think we are too educated to fold bulletins. We may think we are too impatient to work with children. We may think we are above doing certain tasks. Or we may think we aren't smart enough, biblically knowledgeable enough, or godly enough to do certain acts of service. The bottom line is we don't have to be completely capable to serve God, we just have to be willing.

Question Ten

When our attitude for service is to receive a reward from men, then we will be sadly disappointed, both here on earth and in heaven. Jesus warned against this motivation in Matthew 6:1-4.

Our incentive for serving is very important. When we serve to receive the accolades of others, or to make ourselves feel better, the reward will be fleeting. It will not truly satisfy the desires of our heart to please God. God desires our service to be a natural outpouring of our gratitude: "Since we have a kingdom nothing can destroy, let us please God by serving him with thankful hearts and with holy fear and awe" (Hebrews 12:28, LB).

Question Eleven

That night in the Upper Room there were no servants to wash the guests' feet, and none of the disciples volunteered to perform this act. Normally, the washing of the feet would have occurred before the meal had begun. However, Jesus got up in the middle of the meal to offer the service. Perhaps He waited to see if anyone else might make the first move to serve.

This omission of social etiquette revealed more about the disciples' hearts than mere lack of courtesy. Their lack of service showed their desire to be served. Jesus knew their hearts and knew they needed a lesson in how a leader should act.

If you enjoyed this study, be sure to check out other studies in the Kingdom Living series at ampelonpublishing.com

such as ...
"Worship: Nearing the Heart of God"